This book belongs to

_____

OAKY
RUNS A RACE

ATHOL WILLIAMS

Illustrated by Taryn Lock

THEART
Press

OAKY RUNS A RACE
Athol Williams

FIRST EDITION

Published in South Africa by Theart Press
www.theartpressbooks.com
Copyright © ATHOL WILLIAMS 2018
www.atholwilliams.com

Illustrated by Taryn Lock
Book design by Theart Press

ISBN: 978-0-6399373-0-4

Oaky and his acorn friends were playing in their playground. They were rolling on the grass and running among the flowers and trees.

1

A group of pine cones approached the acorns.

"Hey acorns!" one of the pine cones shouted. He sounded gruff and unfriendly.

The acorns stopped playing.

"Which one of you runs the fastest?" the pine cone asked.

All the acorns knew that Oaky was the fastest acorn in all the land.

"I run the fastest," Oaky said.

"I challenge you to a race," the pine cone said to Oaky. "If I win, this will become our playground. If you win, you can stay here and we will leave."

"We don't have to race," Oaky said.
"We can share this playground,
there is lots of space for all of us."

"No!" said the pine cone,
"we want this playground."

The acorns were not happy. They did not want to leave their playground.

The acorns told Oaky to race the pine cone, and Oaky agreed.

The pine cone was much bigger than Oaky but Oaky was not afraid.

Oaky and the pine cone lined up at the starting line. On one side all the acorns were singing:

Go Oaky go
Don't be slow
Be like lightning
Go! Go! Go!

On the other side the pine cones stood quietly.

Oaky said out loud,
"On your marks, get set, GO!"

Oaky and the pine cone were off.
The race was on.

The pine cone dashed into the lead taking huge steps. Oaky's short legs moved slowly and he could only take small steps.

Oaky enjoyed running and ran as fast as he could, but soon he was far behind the pine cone.

Acorns stood all along the way
cheering for Oaky and
singing:

Go Oaky go
Don't be slow
Be like lightning
Go! Go! Go!

Hearing the acorns sing made
Oaky smile and motivated him to
keep running.

The pine cone laughed at Oaky because he was so slow.

Oaky didn't care, he just kept running as fast as he could.

17

Soon the pine cone was so far ahead that Oaky could not see him.

Oaky kept on running.

As Oaky came around a corner, he saw the pine cone sitting on the ground. He had fallen and was crying.

"What should I do?"
Oaky thought to himself.

"If I keep running, I will win the race
and we can keep our playground.
I do like our playground.
If I stop to help the pine cone, he
may run ahead and win the race.
Then we will lose our playground.
What should I do?"

Oaky could see that the pine cone was hurt and decided not to leave him there, so Oaky stopped to help him.

Oaky helped the pine cone to stand. Oaky put his arm around the pine cone and the pine cone's arm around him. Together they started running again.

The pine cone was leaning on Oaky but Oaky didn't mind.

Oaky and the pine cone crossed the finish line together.

No one won the race.

"Thank you for helping me finish the race Oaky," the pine cone said, "when I fell and hurt myself you could have left me there, but you didn't. Even though I was horrible to you, you have shown me friendship."

Oaky smiled at the pine cone and said, "Friendship is more important than winning."

All the acorns were proud of their friend because Oaky had shown kindness and friendship to the pine cone.

"We will leave now," the pine cone said.

"Wait," said Oaky, "we have so much space here. There is enough space for us all to play. You are my new friend. You are all our new friends. Please stay."

The pine cones were happy to hear what Oaky said and smiled for the first time.

So the pine cones stayed.

The acorns and the pine cones played together in the playground, rolling on the grass and running between the flowers and trees.

The End

OAKY RUNS A RACE

Do you know the answers?

1. Who is the fastest acorn? _____

2. What does the pine cone challenge the fastest acorn to do? _____

3. What would happen if the pine cone won the race? _____

    _____

4. When the acorns sing to Oaky "Be like lightning" – what do they mean? _____

    _____

5. What does the word "motivated" mean? (Page 14) _____

    _____

6. Who helped the pine cone when he fell? _____

7. Who won the race? _____

8. What caused all the pine cones to smile? _____

9. The big pine cone was first horrible to Oaky but then became Oaky's friend.

    What did Oaky do to make this happen? _____

    _____

10. According to Oaky, what is more important than winning? _____

    _____

The OAKY Series

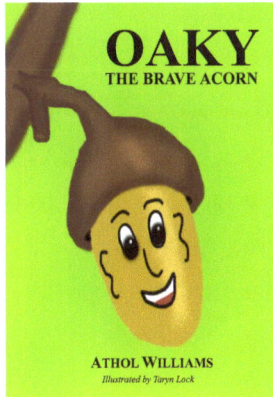

OAKY
THE BRAVE ACORN
ATHOL WILLIAMS
Illustrated by Taryn Lock

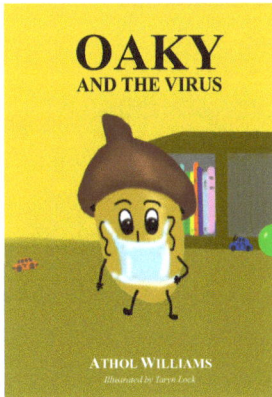

OAKY
AND THE VIRUS
ATHOL WILLIAMS
Illustrated by Taryn Lock

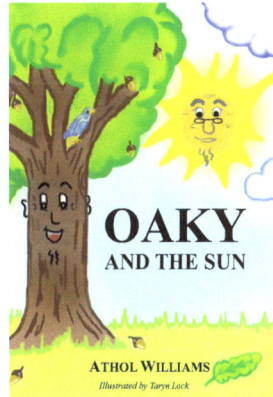

OAKY
AND THE SUN
ATHOL WILLIAMS
Illustrated by Taryn Lock

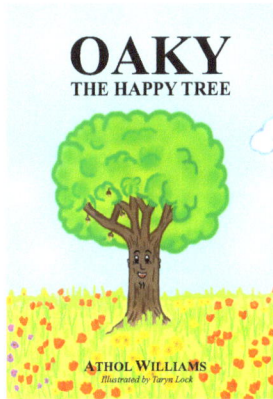

OAKY
THE HAPPY TREE
ATHOL WILLIAMS
Illustrated by Taryn Lock

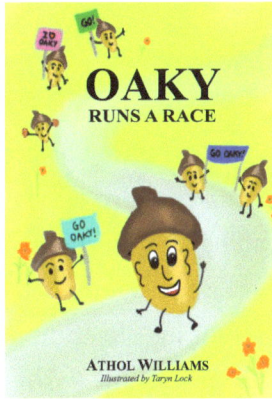

OAKY
RUNS A RACE
ATHOL WILLIAMS
Illustrated by Taryn Lock

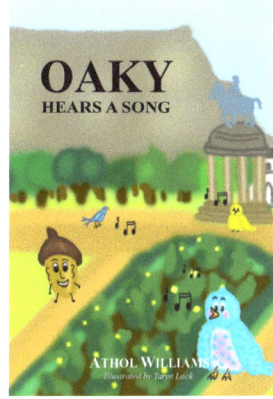

OAKY
HEARS A SONG
ATHOL WILLIAMS
Illustrated by Taryn Lock

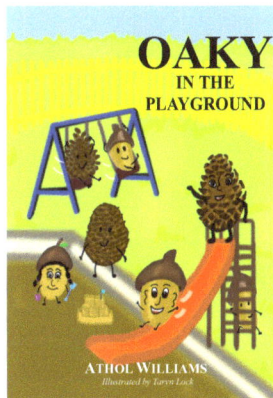

OAKY
IN THE
PLAYGROUND
ATHOL WILLIAMS
Illustrated by Taryn Lock

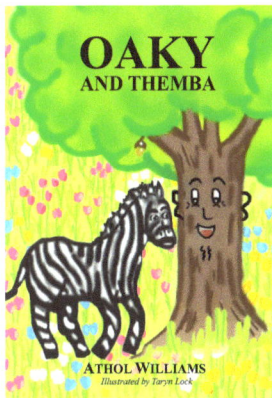

OAKY
AND THEMBA
ATHOL WILLIAMS
Illustrated by Taryn Lock

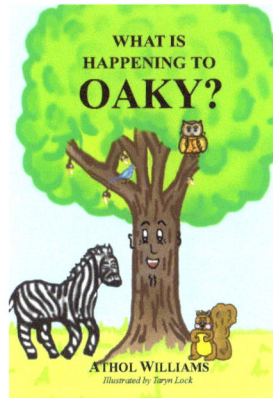

WHAT IS
HAPPENING TO
OAKY?
ATHOL WILLIAMS
Illustrated by Taryn Lock

www.theartpressbooks.com

![READ to RISE logo]

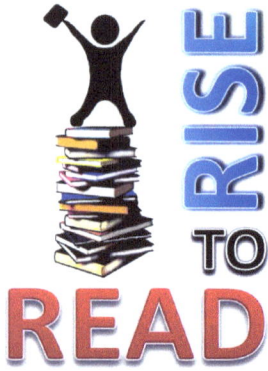

READ to RISE is a registered non-profit organisation committed to promoting literacy among South Africa's youth. As our name suggests, we believe that every child needs to be able to read to rise in their personal development and contribution to society. We adopt a community-centred approach by working in primary schools in selected under-resourced communities.

Our main aims are to inspire children to read and to make high quality books available to them, including books that they get to own. We do not just drop these books off at schools, rather we visit classrooms to conduct our custom-designed interactive classroom programmes. Our classroom programmes are based on the OAKY books which is a series of brightly illustrated, fun reading books that provide valuable lessons and inspirational messages.

Athol Williams, *Author*

I am a poet, social philosopher and corporate advisor. I grew up in Mitchells Plain, Cape Town and I've also lived in Johannesburg, Boston, London and Oxford. I love reading and learning – I have earned six university degrees and received awards for poetry, academic performance and community service. I also love writing – in addition to the OAKY books I have published poetry and my autobiography, *Pushing Boulders.*

Taryn Lock, *Illustrator*

Born and raised in Johannesburg, with an honours degree in Mathematics from the University of the Witwatersrand. I am passionate about promoting literacy by helping people of all ages to read, write and speak - this is the foundation to knowledge and education. I am honoured to illustrate the OAKY series. Through my illustrations, I hope to help writers tell their stories more powerfully.

www.ingramcontent.com/pod-product-compliance
Lightning Source LLC
Chambersburg PA
CBHW042102040426
42448CB00002B/111

9780639937304